ISBN 978-1-334-02837-3
PIBN 10579067

English
Français
Deutsche
Italiano
Español
Português

www.forgottenbooks.com

Mythology Photography **Fiction**
Fishing Christianity **Art** Cooking
Essays Buddhism Freemasonry
Medicine **Biology** Music **Ancient**
Egypt Evolution Carpentry Physics
Dance Geology **Mathematics** Fitness
Shakespeare **Folklore** Yoga Marketing
Confidence Immortality Biographies
Poetry **Psychology** Witchcraft
Electronics Chemistry History **Law**
Accounting **Philosophy** Anthropology
Alchemy Drama Quantum Mechanics
Atheism Sexual Health **Ancient History**
Entrepreneurship Languages Sport
Paleontology Needlework Islam
Metaphysics Investment Archaeology
Parenting Statistics Criminology
Motivational

MR. *BENTLEY*'s

ARTILLERY ELECTION

S E R M O N.

SERMON,

PREACHED BEFORE

THE

ANCIENT AND HONOURABLE

ARTILLERY COMPANY,

IN 𝕭𝖔𝖘𝖙𝖔𝖓,

J U N E 6, 1796,

BEING THE

A N N I V E R S A R Y

OF THEIR

𝕰𝖑𝖊𝖈𝖙𝖎𝖔𝖓 𝖔𝖋 𝕺𝖋𝖋𝖎𝖈𝖊𝖗𝖘.

By WILLIAM BENTLEY, *A. M.*

PASTOR OF THE SECOND CONGREGATIONAL CHURCH IN SALEM.

Ὁπόλεμος τοῖς μὲν δικαίοις ἀναγκαῖος.   MAX. TYR.

BOSTON :
Printed by MANNING & LORING.

1796.

A

S E R M O N.

PROVERBS xxx. 5, 6.

EVERY WORD OF GOD IS PURE:
HE IS A SHIELD UNTO THEM THAT PUT THEIR TRUST IN HIM.
ADD THOU NOT UNTO HIS WORDS;
LEST HE REPROVE THEE, AND THOU BE FOUND A LIAR.

THIS valuable fragment from the records of ancient wifdom, comprehends this ufeful truth, that from experience are all our fafe conclufions, refpecting the character of fociety, and the happinefs to be attained in it. The refolution formed upon this maxim, has been more celebrated, than the maxim itfelf. It is experience which recommends moderation in our defires, and in our expectations, but facts, in all ages, are more eafily communicated by words, than the maxims, which juftify the conclufions of our higheft wifdom. The writer affirms, that independent of every advantage from genius and education,

cation, this truth of our text is eſtabliſhed. The whole paragraph contains an appeal* of a man to his neighbours, or an inquiry which may be thus repreſented. Indeed, ſhould I have no uncommon natural powers; or ſhould I not have cultivated my underſtanding; ſhould I not have been a man of deep reflection, or ſhould I not have the ſecrets of inſpiration; tell me, whence could I get wiſdom? Am I firſt to comprehend all creation? Who hath done this? Who hath aſcended into heaven, or who hath deſcended? Who hath gathered the winds in his hand, or confined the waters in his garment? Who hath eſtabliſhed all parts of the earth? What is the name of this man, or what is his ſon's name? Can any man tell? Is not every truth of God approved, when it has been ſafe to thoſe who truſt in it? Add thou not then raſhly to his words; affirm only from experience; left thy folly be expoſed, and thou lead other men into errour. He then proceeds to his concluſion. He had conſidered affluence, and poverty, and had devoutly obſerved how far they contribute uſually to happineſs, and he tells us, that experience and obſervation had reconciled his mind to the nature of human life, and had taught him to acquieſce in thoſe moderate deſires, which are much more adapted to health, and contentment, and have their objects commonly within every man's reach. Experience has continued to decide in favour of this choice, and to render it happy. Our text then aſſures us that the laws of God are known from experience, and from the ſafety and happineſs men find in them; that every advantage beyond paſt experience, ſhould be purſued with the greateſt caution; that attempts at higher

happineſs

* Theie is a different preface in the Vulgate.

happiness have been made with frequent disappointments ; that reformations have been urged, but not accomplished ; and that the many disappointments should be lessons of the highest wisdom to mankind.

This sentiment accommodates itself to the present solemnities. The horrours of war are to be deprecated. Benevolence teaches us to avoid them ; found policy to prevent them by all reasonable measures ; and religion to abhor the occasions of them. But the world is not in our power. Passions exist every where, beyond control from principles within, and from fears without. General happiness is the best object of political economy, and should be regarded in all laws and in every community. But it is not what exists, but what is to be pursued. It is to the mind, an assemblage of all those blessings, which have been reported among men, but which have never existed together, or in perfection. The picture is bold. It may fill the mind, and inspire sublime hopes. But steadily viewed, and without fair comparison with nature, it may distract the imagination, make men forget the proportions of nature, and leave them dissatisfied with the real objects before them, and with that happiness, which is their best, because their highest attainment. But even this happiness is unequal in different nations, and in different ages. Its progress in society resembles the progress of all our knowledge from experience. It is gained by slow degrees and calm inquiry, and it is accompanied with unavoidable prejudices. Nations like men have a resemblance in their general character, but their manners may be distinct. The reestablishment of any police has been found to be impracticable, because the habits, which formed it, are unattainable.

unattainable. Nations may profit by the refemblance, becaufe they knew from it the objeƈt of government and the charaƈter of mankind. But no hopes from experience will rife above the condition of human nature. From the wifdom of preceding ages,* Mofes fupplied the principles of his government, and the leffons of morality which accompany his laws. He did not inftitute wars, but he found them in the order of our world. He did not reafon about their nature, but their coincidence with his political hopes. The political exiftence of his nation began, when they were in arms. The principles upon which they were taken at firft, were never unneceffary, nor was their influence upon the national charaƈter ever loft. They reduced moral life below the ftandard of an happy government, but the people had not the fpirit of fuch a government. There are in times of peace, inftitutions of as aƈtive virtue, and of as high fpirit of honour, as can exift in war. There may exift a generous emulation in the arts, and of civil honours, which may command all the refources of human genius. And there are the endearing manners of domeftic life to fweeten the temper, and to conciliate the affeƈtions. It was not, becaufe upon fair comparifon, war could be preferred, but becaufe war was more congenial with the prevalent charaƈter of mankind. The fpirit of war fpeaks in the devotion of David. But his fublime thoughts could not infpire thofe emotions, which compofe the defcription of wifdom by his fucceffour. It was in the quiet of a peaceful eftablifhment, that the age became enlightened, as well as great. But in our world, we have not been able to provide the events, which combine

* Spencer.

bine empires, and preferve their exiftence, otherwife than by the active and contending paffions of mankind. Thefe events have not only given being to all great nations, but they have aided the triumph of every religious eftablifhment. Even religious wars have ever been worfe than thofe of princes for civil caufes, or political fame, becaufe they have more paffion, and it is determined from the origin and nature of the eftablifhments, confequent upon them, that they cannot be the foundation for the hopes of a perpetual peace. The difference of motives profeffed in them, has made no difference in the enormities, they have occafioned. It then remains a queftion, fince fuch a ftate of the paffions has ever exifted, as is a felf-exciting caufe of war, and therefore as its incentives cannot fail from the prefent conftitution of the human mind, whether a ftate of conftant preparation, be not the only ftate of fafety, to nations, and to mankind.

To examine a fubject of this interefting nature, we muft not propofe a favourite theory of the paffions, but fome example of the moft happy conduct of them. If we cannot find a fuccefsful experiment, we fhould produce the beft effects in circumftances, moft indulgent to our hopes. We fhould examine the minds of men, when moft detached from the political views of their age, fimple in their manners, elevated beyond the love of fame, or wealth, and in their maxims pure, peaceable, and fubmiffive. Too humble to hope for preferment in the ftate, and too devout to refufe the moft fevere reftraints upon their paffions. From the conduct of fuch men, we may judge of the influence of condition, of the progrefs of fociety, of the motives of profperity, and of the nature of a religious or civil

B   eftablifhment.

eftablifhment. And our conclufions from fuch an ex. ample, may be as fafe, as the nature of human knowl. edge will admit.

And what hiftory can be better adapted to a Chriftian affembly, than the hiftory of their own religion? Chriftians being in civil fociety, did not refufe obedience to the laws. The right of war was not denied, or maintained. The manners they affociated with their religious profeffion, were governed by the love of peace. From the abfence of power, and the full ftrength of mutual dependence, their habits were more focial and more pure. The moft offenfive part of their lives was obliged by perfecution, and their unkind opinions of mankind; but this affifted them in their refiftance to the habits of civil fociety, and for a long time preferved them from the compliances, which gradually obtained from pretended regard to convenience and to duty, and the fuppofed obligations of different circumftances, but really from the affimilation of their manners and character to that of human nature, and the order of our world. This expediency was difclofed in a letter, or in fome guarded expreffion; was betrayed in confidence, and employed with fear; was adopted with caution, and confeffed with diffidence; was oppofed by reftraints and qualifications; before it was eftablifhed in belief, boafted of as juft, and maintained by violence. Chriftians, after long depreffion, voluntary mortifications, and arbitrary rules upon the paffions, and even under the belief of a fpeedy and a miraculous change of condition in our world, at laft claimed and exercifed all the rights of war. They borrowed in their earlieft profperity from every inftitution, which could unite with the preju-

dices

dices of their converts. We look not then at their primitive morals, but at the character of man : not at professions, but at actions. Mahomed adopted war, but the Christians had practised it. Christians yielded to its expediency, but Mahomedans profiting by experience, entered upon the world in triumph.

To trace this history may not be without instruction. The Author of our religion has reported by his disciples, his own convictions of the right of war. Jesus discovered to his friends, before his entrance upon the garden, in which he was apprehended, that he was determined to resist. But the prudence of a disciple could not be as easily under the command of his master, as his zeal. The reproof assures him, that his resistance was unseasonable, not unlawful ; because he went armed by his authority, and with his knowledge. His followers were thus taught to employ prudence with the lawfulness of war : And as the destruction of the country was impending, they were not taught to contend in its battles. This ingenuous temper was not lost in the primitive ages. To our own times, the records of men, who were governed by their religion, rather than education, have been carefully transmitted. A work attributed to one* of the first Christians, dissuades from sedition and schism, from moral motives, rather than from express and religious prohibition. And from military arrangements, he happily illustrates the common interest, which comprehends what is useful to the strength and defence of their cause. A care for personal safety induces another† to advise to appease the people, from a knowledge of their passions, which precipitate human affairs.

---

* Clement.　　　　　　† Ignatius.

fairs. While a third* qualifies his obedience to civil authority by the protection, he receives ; and from the indignation which rifes againſt inſult and oppreſſion, he claims the right to queſtion their power, who do public wrongs. The character and the juſtice of theſe feelings, in our free government, it is not neceſſary to vindicate, or deſcribe. They belong to the beſt part of human nature.

In the next period we fee leſs ſimplicity of heart, and leſs ingenuous ſentiments. When Chriſtianity had a public form, and a riſing intereſt, it ſpeaks in flattering apologies, from its more learned friends, the language of the laws, and the ſubordination of the empire. Thus while one† acquieſces in the laws of ſlavery, and the full authority oˡ reaſon, and government in the concerns of life, another‡ to quiet the ſtate, aſcribes falſe honours tc his religion, and profeſſes to prefer prayers to arms, and in the apparent piety, though errour of his addreſs, he oppoſes active duty to devotion, and the order of civil ſociety, to the hopes of a divine religion. While a third,§ more ſincere, than diſcerning, dares to anticipate a triumph over the laws of nature, from an authority not eſtabliſhed in theſe laws, but formed in a religion too pure to exiſt in the preſent order of our world. But the patrons of the Chriſtian cauſe, were not all of this character. They had refined their taſte by the elegance of Rome, and had imbibed the manners of ſociety with the beſt knowledge of its laws. They were not ſo ignorant as to plead for war from virtue, or religion, nor ſo ſuperſtitious, as to ſubvert ſociety, by refuſing it the neceſſary defence. To the paſſions of
life,

---

* Polycarp.　　† Athenagoras.　　‡ Juſtin.　　§ Irenæus.

life, and to the habits of civil-fociety, they imputed the convulfions of empires, and the defence of the fword. To meliorate human condition, it was taught,* that the paffions muft be governed. That from their natural character, human genius was difplayed in the arts of military defence, as well as in the maxims of virtue. The difputes of the age† for power, and the vile fervices of faction were ftigmatized, as unlawful to Chriftians from a regard to reputation and the public peace, while Roman eloquence in the fchool of Chrift, taught the philofophy of reafon and religion. "Nor do I refufe," fays an enlightened Chriftian,‡ " to confefs, that it is the duty of man to know himfelf in all the relations of his being. What he is, whence he is, and why he exifts. This duty he cannot perform, without an inquiry into all things around him, for they are fo affociated, connected, and united, that an ignorance of them involves an ignorance of himfelf, and difqualifies him for every civil obligation. Where is fociety formed on virtue," he appeals, " or diffolved without blood ? Wars throughout the world, difunite the deareft kindred, and the greateft empires report not the fame biftory of their fate !"

A caufe, which could admit fuch rational views of fociety, muft have already rifen into reputation, and its friends muft have had an acquaintance with the world. We may then foon expect to find its power and its influence employed in public affairs. When Chriftianity had thus prevailed, its friends had intereft at court, and in the armies. It had a command among parties in the ftate. Experience has told us, what to expect. Let us hear, how the Fathers reafon, what the

---

* Lactantius.   † Tertullian.   ‡ Minutius Felix.

the councils publish, and the civil laws ordain. Let us liften to Chryfoftom, who exalted the glory of a Chriftian prince, and to a Gregory who pleaded with bold imagination and genius againft an apoftate. We may find perpetuated the profperity of an eftablifhment, by all the means of civil power, till a Bernard difplays to us the full force of profperity upon a long continued fuperftition, which had eftablifhed itfelf upon the pureft religion ever profeffed among men. We behold at length a war which armed Europe, and was the boldeft effort of paffion in religion. Conqueft was authorifed in the caufe of religion, and the power of war, the conduct of armies, and the control of the civil government were furrendered to its claims.

At firft, to engage Chriftians in war, the crofs was difplayed in their banners. This was not fo great a ftruggle with former prejudices as we might imagine. No fect had prevailed, which had been under the imputation of making war unlawful. All reports leave reafonable fears of mifconftruction upon their opinion. The myftic fects in their infancy might favour or incline to it. Chriftians fought, at an early period, promotion to civil and military honours, and gradually acquired their influence in the empire. Even the dignities in the church did not extinguifh all claims, or prove fufficient to gratify their ambition, and the excefs of panegyric, was the reward of the civil Fathers for diftinctions, which they readily beftowed. A canon early impofed a reftraint upon this ambition. From the modeft vindication of felf defence in former apologies, the eloquence of Chryfoftom proceeds to compare the mind under its paffions, to a body in a fever, in which fafety directs the remedy. To a Chriftian

tian teacher he not only infinuates, but recommends an addrefs devoid of Chriftian fimplicity. The power of princes was an emblem of fpiritual dominion, too flattering not to be indulged. The Chriftians had fought too many battles, and with too great fuccefs, to doubt of the divine right of power, or the lawfulnefs of war. And, though Chriftian teachers were profeffed friends of peace, they had profited enough from affairs of ftate, to know what the Bifhop affured them was true, that excellence in political knowledge was a commendable qualification. An emperour averfe from the power and name of a Chriftian foon found the reluctance with which honours were abandoned. Panegyric was converted into the moft bitter invective. The praifes of Conftantine from Chryfoftom may be oppofed to the talents of Gregory againft Julian. Whatever could irritate by comparifon, or be hateful in its motives, or injurious to reputation was pronounced without referve. A fpirit fo freely encouraged in the primates of any order, cannot be reftrained by any inftitutions. Neither the habit of a reclufe, nor his vows will confine his ambition. The pride of opinion is not obftinate againft the temptations of power. Enemies are more eafily filenced by authority, than argument. The great Auguftin encouraged the temper. In defiance of his firft maxims, he paffed from a vindication of war, to the command of God in it. He pronounced that the general, or the foldier were not fo much authors of war, as the minifters of God, and that they might exult, Bleffed be the Lord, who teacheth our hands to war, and our fingers to fight.

Thus at laft orders eftablifhed to exhibit the virtues of retirement and filence, became powerful affociations

in

in the church, and were transformed into ſtanding.
armies, to inſtigate reſentment, and to interfere in the
political concerns of princes. When the church became eſtabliſhed, there were few fears entertained upon the ſubject of war, among the ruling ecclefiaſtics.
The former doubts aroſe in private condition, in humble ſects, and in times of perſecution, but they diſap-
peared among even good men, when they were ac-
quainted with the neceſſity impoſed upon our world,
whatever peaceful diſpoſitions they wiſhed to cultivate
in it. They found it vain to ſtruggle againſt the
order of events, and that their prudence and their
ſtrength confiſted in that conſtant preparation, which
could render them formidable to their enemies. The
ſame extenſive views of life, which exalt the hopes of
virtue, obliged thoſe guards againſt the paſſions, which
appear as clearly in the laws, the polity and education
of every country, as they do in their military arrangements.

We may then confider the experiment upon the
Chriſtian world as fairly made, and believe that no
means have been found, to render its true principles ſo general and active, as to render our prepara-
tions for war unneceſſary. And no ſucceſs will juſti-
fy our expectations of univerſal peace till public order,
is public ſentiment, rather than law, which at preſent
appears to be a period, as remote from this, as any
former age. Nor is the Chriſtian a ſolitary experiment. The military is the beſt defined part of the in-
ſtitution of Moſes. The equeſtrian order of Rome is
better underſtood than the Senate ; and the abuſe of
the military power, is the moſt notorious errour of the
feudal

feudal fyftem. An order of patriots* arofe out of our late revolution, whom our national honour and fafety teach us to reverence. And the inftitution we honour this day, reminds us of a more early military affociation. And fuch parts of our excellent federal conftitution have proved to be the moft found, which have wifely regarded principles, it was obliged to admit and indulge, more from the wifdom and experience of nations, than from our own immediate preference or choice.

But left we fhould diftruft the zeal of ancient times, and prefume upon modern wifdom, we have before us in our own country, the moft bold experiment, ever made in favour of perpetual peace, and it was conducted upon the Chriftian motives of piety and benevolence.

A fect eftablifhed upon the lovely plea, that it was practicable to live without war, originated a ftate of civil fociety in a new country. The power of the magiftrate, it did admit, and did attempt to define. Says the moft able apologift† of the fect, " Let it be admitted that the magiftrate may lawfully ufe his authority to preferve moral and perpetual ftatutes." He then prefumes that every thing is granted, which ought to be required. But if laws may require the virtues of obedience, they muft defend the obedient. And the means of defence muft be as extenfive as the evils of oppofition. The means muft be adequate. But in what does any penalty differ effentially from a war ? To find the point at which men may defift, fhort of the extent of their power, is difficult. If the

C   individual

* Cincinnati.   † Barclay.

individual may be defended, the ftate muft be, which unites its fafety with the multitude of the people. Civil fociety involves then the right of war. But when we obferve the expedients to promote this falfe fecurity of fociety ; when we fee its abject depend- ence ; when we behold the character of intereft in it ; the limited power, or rather equivocal nature of its government, depending on private manners ; the fu- periour ftrength of private will ; the difcouragement of knowledge to preferve it, the dangers of ambition; and the reluctant acquiefcence in this ftate, the for- did interefts it creates in multiplied private views, and when we add an impartial* view of facts, which are of the greateft confequence, the experiment appears con- trary to nature, to civil government, and to perfonal fafety.

But while we confefs the neceffity of war, and of a ftate of defence, we ought to be cautious not to pro- pofe too freely political advantages from war, or to encourage a difpofition to provoke it, without a faered regard to all the motives of an honourable peace. There is an ambition, which may be awakened in great revolutions, but it fhould have urgent and noble occafions. Dangers may provoke rafhnefs, rather than courage. Wars are eafily converted into real evils. Conquefts have been faithfully reported, and hiftory dwells upon them, but ambition for war has been often fatal. If wars can raife the fame of na- tions, they can as powerfully concur with the means of their deftruction. The confequences of the Pelo- ponnefian war upon the Grecian ftates, have been con- feffed, and deplored. The ftate in which Grecian arts flourifhed, was of peace.

The

---

* Smith's Letters on Pennfylvania.

The ambition of Rome under a military government employed a rivalfhip, which had glory, but not victory, and fhews how powerfully the felf infpiration of liberty unites with excellence in the arts beyond the love of the arts, when aided only by power. A more generous emulation and friendfhip of the arts in Europe prevented the recurrence of the fame events. Independent nations produced a principle more active than any motives of government, and genius employed the moft fplendid advantages, and was triumphant. And we ought on this occafion, to pay a juft tribute of refpect to that patriot,* who juftly holds a diftinguifhed office in our federal government, for that feafonable work, in which he has placed before us, the political experience of our world. Could the higheft wifdom have chofen a fubject, could it have chofen a better for the inftruction and glory of our country? It affords a review of the difficulties of civil government, and of the endlefs expedients to maintain the profperity of ftates. Convinced of the nature of war, men in all ages, have imagined, that they could act upon their fober convictions: They have attempted to inftitute an higher order of things, and to create an influence of opinion over the paffions of the world.

But they who confider the prefent ftate of our world, and our conftant experience in it, may find the neceffity of that fublime religion, which inftructs our prudence in this world, but eftablifhes our beft hopes upon our qualifications for a better life, and they may increafe their efteem of that revelation upon which all our hopes of happinefs muft reft. Our higheft duty is to guard againft impending evils, while we endeavour

* JOHN ADAMS,

our to preferve from a love of the public happinefs, for our own times, the fweet intervals of peace, in the wifdom of our laws, and in our conftant preparation for a moft active defence.

To correct the vanity of our expectations from the greater wifdom to prevail in our world from any caufes, which now exift in it, let us only recollect the caufes, which have already proved infufficient to eftablifh a more happy order of things. Genius has in every country had its opportunities, to affift a flourifhing age, and to plead with mankind, in favour of the bleffings of peace. When princes have contributed to the lovely purpofe, the public fentiment of joy has been addreffed to them in the boldeft panegyric. But the ambition of ftatefmen, the corrupt manners, and turbulent paffions of men have interrupted and fruftrated every generous defign to eftablifh, what men have profeffed to believe to be the dignity of life and the end of government. Religion alfo has given its friendly affiftance. But violence has been nurfed even at the altars, and they who for one age affociated religion with peace, have refigned it to thofe, who have made it the incentive of war. The human faculties continue to develop unequally. Ambition is not lefs ftrong, as the advantages of education are extended. Natural and untutored paffions with all their incentives, every where exift. War has yet all its caufes. The paffions which excite it, it can inflame. Little durable happinefs then can we hope from the enthufiafm of mankind in the moft ardent love of liberty. They feel their native claims on liberty, but command not for a long time, the wifdom to preferve it.

it. In the means of bold refiftance nations become formidable, and reftrain their enemies.

With fincerity then, we congratulate the Members of this ANCIENT AND HONOURABLE ARTILLERY COMPANY affembled this day, in the fpirit of our anceftors, who were urged by a love of liberty and religion to eftablifh themfelves in thefe remote, and uncultivated regions. The rigour of their manners formed by perfecution, and confirmed by habits of fuffering, and danger, did not inftruct them, with an ingenious modern,* 'that the biftory of the Jews was not an example to them, or that local manners were the true principles of Chriftian morality. They conceived that their future hopes did not refufe them the beft means to fecure their prefent fafety, and they affociated the ufe of arms, with their pureft doctrines. Like Mofes, they fupplied laws from experience, and like the great teacher of their religion, they provided principles of active virtue in the moft humble condition. In this inftitution and fchool of arms, we recover the biftory of their beft families, as well as principles, and the names of the officers lead us to the recollection of men, who have been confpicuous in the fucceffive generations from the plantation of the colony, to the prefent flourifhing ftate of our commonwealth. It tranfmits the character and the fentiments of Maffachufetts. As a very early inftitution it demands our veneration. In its freedom from innovation it is a memorial of the ftability of the public opinion regarding the ufe of arms ; and even with its interruptions, it records its intimate connexion with the liberties of the people. During the laft efforts

of

* Soame Jenyns.

of the Houfe of Stuarts to perpetuate their power, it ceafed to enjoy its privileges, and in our late war with the parent country, it gave place to the eftablifhment of an army. Its members faw at thefe memorable periods, the boldeft attempts for freedom. In the firft, the fpirit of revolution was directed by an ambition devoid of principle, and by an enthufiafm which could command, but not enjoy victory. Its ftrength proved the terrour of a government, it was not able to reform, and fear qualified a power, which was not abfolutely withdrawn. But in the other we beheld, the mild virtues infpired by the love of liberty and mankind, and guarded by prudence and fortitude, conducted to victory by the laws of a free people. Our General became immortal, and our caufe yet triumphs in the federal conftitution, and in the peace and profperity of our country. Thus have the abfent years of the biftory of this inftitution been fupplied from the records of our nation, as faered to courage, and to a glorious defence of arms in the hands of a free people. Its prefent worthy members, and officers* its active patriots, and the commanders of our late army perpetuate its fame. The names of a HULL, a BROOKS, and a LINCOLN will be reverenced in future ages. May our national defence be as perfect, as it is neceffary, and juft.

But mankind are yet in a ftate of war. How terrible has been the havoc among the moft enlightened nations of Europe! We confefs the melancholy truth. And we will not fall a willing facrifice to the paffions of angry nations. We love peace, but we will render
it

* Q. M. Gen. AMASA DAVIS, Commander of the Company. J. EATON, Lieutenant. JER. KANLER, Enfign.

it fafe and honourable. We defire to poffefs the beft bleffings of civil government, but we will be able to defend it. To reftrain the paffions of men, we muft be a terrour to them. We will love peace, but we will defy ambition, hate oppreffion, and die for our laws and our liberty. Pure religion will teach us to love peace, and experience will teach us, how to pre-ferve it. But we will never forget that the good citi-zen is a good foldier. Able to defend, as well as fure to deferve his liberty. He hates faction, but he is not afraid of war in defence of his country. He loves peace, becaufe it preferves the higheft value of freedom. He rifes to conquer perverfe paffions, not to employ them in his own caufe. He appears to fup-port the laws, not to triumph over them. His victory is for good government, and to God, with a pure confcience, he can commit his caufe.